CW00850663

THE RUNNING JOKES
BY ULTRA TIM DAVIS

This book is dedicated to humor that can be involved in both running and ultrarunning. Both runners and non-runners will be able to find laughter at various situations posed here.

What is a running joke? The basic definition of a running joke is something that a group of people continue to refer to and find funny over a period of time. These running jokes will focus on actual jokes about running or not running, as the case may be.

TABLE OF CONTENTS

CHAPTER 1 - Q & A

(A) OK - Good Running Jokes

Q: Why do runners go jogging early in the morning?
A: They want to finish before their brain figures out what they're doing.

Q: What do you call a free treadmill?
A: Outside.

Q: What do a dentist and a track coach have in common?
A: They both use drills!

Q: How do crazy runners go through the forest?
A: They take the "psycho path"

Q: How do you know if you're a running enthusiast?
A: When you have more running clothes than regular clothes in your laundry pile.

Q: What makes an avid runner get jealous?
A: Seeing other people running when they have to drive somewhere.

Q: Why can't you take a nap during a race?
A: Because if you snooze, you lose!

Q: How do you know you're a dedicated runner?
A: When your treadmill has more miles on it than your car.

Q: Why did the trainer want her client to work out where it was sunny?
A: So she would feel the burn.

Q: What do you call a competitive runner who just broke up with his girlfriend?
A: Homeless

Q: What kind of running shoes are made from banana skins?
A: Slippers.

Q: What do you get when you run in front of a car?
A: TIRED

Q: What do you get when you run behind a car?
A: EXHAUSTED

(B) Bad - Worse Running Jokes

Q: What do runners do when they forget something?
A: They jog their memory

Q: Why can't you let a jogger be a potential juror?
A: Because you'll have a runaway jury.

Q: What do you call running while listening to your favorite rapper?
A: A Snoop Jogg.

Q: Who is the fastest runner of all time?
A: Adam, because he came first in the human race!

Q: Did you hear about the race between the lettuce and the tomato?
A: The lettuce was a "head" and the tomato was trying to "ketchup"!

Q: If twenty monkeys run after one banana, what time is it?
A: Twenty after one!

Q: Why did the chicken run across the road?
A: There was a car coming.

Q: If runners get athlete's foot what do astronauts get?
A: Mistletoe

Q: If I cut Usain Bolt what am I?
A: A bolt cutter.

Q: Why did the vegetarians stop running cross country?
A: They didn't like meets!

Q: Did you hear about the marathon runner who ran for three hours but only moved two feet?
A: He only had two feet!

Q: What race is never run?
A: A swimming race.

Q: How did the barber win the foot race?
A: He took a "shortcut"

CHAPTER 2 - SHORT RUNNING JOKES

Computer Running Too Slow? - If your computer is slow, paint a Jamaican flag on it and it will run faster.

Why 2 Hunters Raced Each Other: Two hunters are walking through a forest looking for deer. When all of a sudden, a giant bear jumps out and scares the shit out of them. They drop their guns and run like hell. One of the hunters stopped, opened up his backpack and laced up a pair of Running shoes. His buddy looked at him and said, "What are you doing? Are you crazy? You can't outrun the bear!" To this the hunter said, "I know, all I have to do is outrun you!"

Working Out vs. Runner's Highs: "We work out too much. We waste time. A friend of mine runs marathons. He always talks about this "runner's high." But he has to go 26 miles for it. That's why I smoke and drink. I get the same feeling from a flight of stairs."

A Beginner At Jogging (Running Shoes With Pocket): Deciding to take up jogging, the man was astounded by the wide selection of jogging shoes available at the local sports shoe store. While trying on a basic pair of jogging shoes, he noticed a minor feature and asked the clerk: "What is this little pocket thing here on the side for?" And the clerk: "Oh, that's to carry spare change so you can call your wife to come pick you up when you've jogged too far."

World Record 100M Dash: An athlete has just broken the world record in the one hundred meters. All the other runners come to congratulate him and hear him murmur, "Like screw the guy who put the baby squirrel in my pants!"

Gas Company Footrace: Two gas company servicemen, an experienced supervisor and a new trainee, were out checking meters in a suburban neighborhood. They parked their truck at the end of the alley and worked their way to the other end. At the last house, a woman looking out her kitchen window watched the two men as they checked her gas meter. Finishing the meter check, the senior supervisor challenged his younger coworker to a foot race down the alley back to the truck to prove that an older guy could outrun a younger one. As they came running up to the truck, they realized the lady from that last house was huffing and puffing right behind them. They stopped and asked her what was wrong. Gasping for breath, she replied "When I see two gas servicemen running as hard as you two were, I figured I'd better run too!"

Good Runner's Advice: Before you criticize someone, you should walk a mile in their shoes. That way, when you criticize them, you're a mile away and you have their shoes.

Sign Posted in a Podiatrist's Office: "Time wounds all heels".

Love: A runner asks his wife: "What do you love most about me? My tremendous athletic ability or my superior intellect?" "What I love most about you," responded the man's wife, "is your running sense of humor."

The Olympic Medalist And The Bouncer (True Story): Michael Johnson, the Olympic Gold Medal runner, was on his way to a club with some friends. At the door the bouncer turned to him and said, "Sorry mate, you can't come in here; no denim allowed." Michael was quite annoyed by this and retorted, "Don't you know who I am? I'm Michael Johnson." To which the bouncer replied, "Then it won't take you long to run home and change."

CHAPTER 3 - RUNNING CARTOONS

BUYING new shoes won't make
you a better runner, but
RUNNING in them will.

RUNNER'S HIGH...
FEELIN' FAST! CAN'T WAIT TO SEE MY TIME!
RUNNER'S LOW...
I FORGOT TO START MY WATCH

Slow runners make
fast runners look good.
YOU'RE WELCOME.

You know you are a runner when...
GONE FOR A RUN .com
You own more pairs of running
shoes than any other type of shoes.

I don't know when I run faster:
When I'm leaving work
so I can get home
to run or when I'm
actually out on
my run?

I don't always run...
But when I do it's
because the swim and
bike didn't kill me...

It's one of those days where if I don't go for a run, you'll be lucky not to see me on the news.

No matter how slow you go, you are still lapping everybody on the couch!

JUST RUN

You know you're a runner when

Your first question to the doctor is
"HOW SOON CAN I GO RUNNING AGAIN"

Most people don't realize
this, but you can run
without telling Facebook
about it.

Whenever I see someone running faster than me I say "They're not going as far" –takes the sting out of it

CHAPTER 4 - MARATHON RUNNING JOKES & MEMES

Injured myself during an Ironman marathon the other day,
Got up too fast after watching the third film

I treat everyday like I'm running a marathon tomorrow...
I rest, don't run and load up on carbs.

My friends won't stop teasing me for giving up in a marathon after only 1 mile;
I've become a running joke

We're always making fun of our friend who threw up during a marathon
It's a running gag.

Why didn't the programmer win a marathon?
He had a runtime error

Wish me luck in the London Marathon today. I managed a respectable 3 hours, 12 minutes, last year...
This year, I will try to beat that but I usually get bored and end up turning over to watch something else...

What does the winner of the Boston Marathon lose?
His breath.

I once finished 2 marathons in 2 minutes.
Then they changed the name to Snickers..

Training for a marathon can be hard work.
But it'll be good for you in the long run.

I don't win Marathons because I'm lucky.
I win because I'm driven.

I'm never again donating a dime to any charity raising funds for a marathon.
They just take the money and run.

When is the best time to run a marathon?
During Lent. That's when you fast.

What types of marathons do racist people run?
Only 3ks

Arnold Schwarzenegger is organizing a marathon to raise money for the rebuild of Notre Dame…
It's slogan is … 'Run with me if you want to give'

What happened to Han when Chewie wouldn't do the marathon?
He Ran Solo…

Did you hear Han Solo will be running next year's London Marathon?
He says he reckons he'll be able to finish in less than 26 miles

Did you hear about the oompah loompah marathon?
Contestants are running short.

Seriously do not mess with a marathoner -
They run the streets!

Why did the marathon runner end up in jail?
For resisting a rest.

The national nude marathon won by a woman for the twentieth year in a row.
In places 2 - 10 was a group of men with no regrets.

"I'm thinking of running a marathon again." I told my friend.
"You've run a marathon before?" she asked, with an air of admiration.
I said, "No, but I've thought about it."

So Doc' Can she run a marathon?
After fixing a young girl's broken bone a father asks "Will she be able to run a marathon when she recovers?"

To which the doctor replied "I don't see why not!"

The dad then says "That's odd, she couldn't run a marathon before!"

Last year I entered a marathon.
The race started and immediately I was the last of the runners. It was embarrassing.

The guy who was in front of me, second to last, was

making fun of me. He said, "Hey buddy, how does it feel to be last?" I replied, "You really want to know?"

Then I dropped out of the race!

I'm getting tired of your Barenaked Ladies marathon.

"It's been one week since you looked at me!"

Do you want to hear a joke about the Boston Marathon?

Never mind. I'll never finish it.

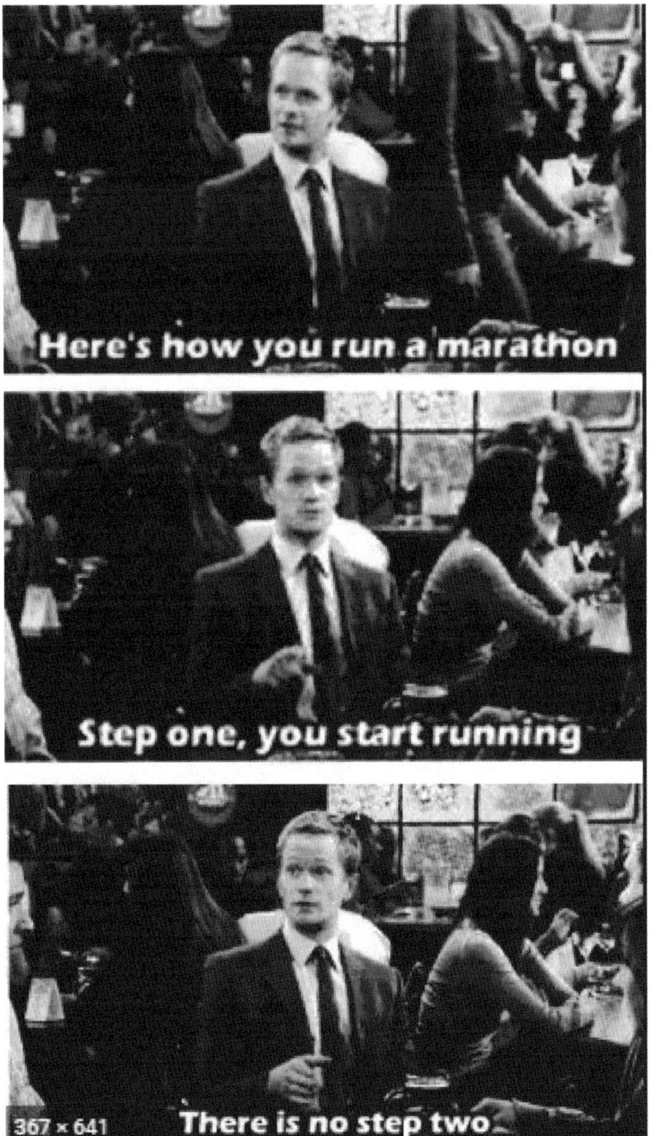
Here's how you run a marathon
Step one, you start running
367 × 641
There is no step two

They said,
Run a Marathon.
It will be fun, they said...

That feeling at whatever mile you start hitting that wall

CHAPTER 5 - FUNNY MARATHON SIGNS

Marathon runners are often plagued by the monotony during the race and funny signs from spectators are always helpful. Keeping a good sense of humor during a race will get you through that marathon more than you think. Here's some of the most popular signs:

1. Run like you stole something

2. I'm sure it seemed like a good idea 10 months ago

3. Worst parade ever

4. You've got stamina! Call me!

5. Pain now…beer later

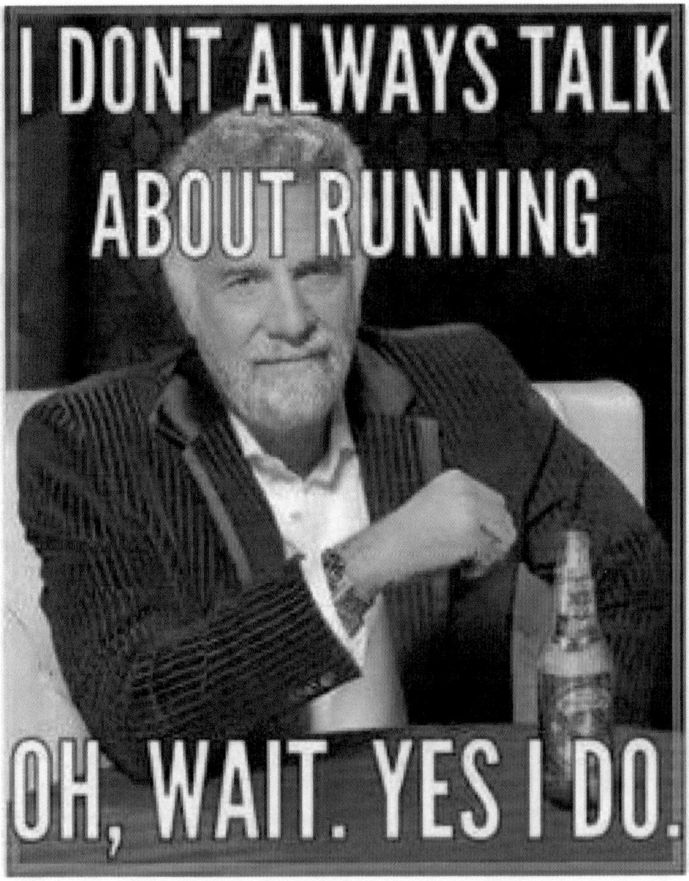
I DONT ALWAYS TALK
ABOUT RUNNING
OH, WAIT. YES I DO.

Plan is to wait until mile 26, call in the lactic acid troops and seize up.
Brilliant!
GONE FOR A RUN .com
1050 × 802

MARATHON ROUTE
HELL
START
PURE HELL
FINISH → GET T-SHIRT AND BANANA
SHEER HELL
UTTER HELL

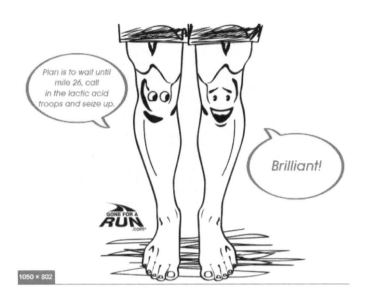

When you get in the shower and realize how badly you chafed.

#RunSelfieRepeat

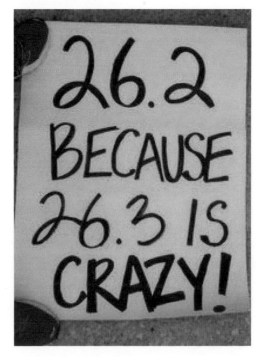

26.2 BECAUSE 26.3 IS CRAZY!

CHAPTER 6 - FUNNY RUNNING SHIRTS

An equally hilarious phenomena are running shirts with quirky or funny messages. Not only can you express your inner-most sarcastic thoughts, everyone else can enjoy it as well. Here are some popular shirt messages:

1. See Dick run. See Jane run faster.

2. Athletes run. Everyone else just plays games.

3. Why are all these people following me?

4. Running is a mental sport…and we're all insane!

5. I run like a girl…try to keep up

CHAPTER 7 - TRAIL RUNNING & ULTRA RUNNING JOKES & CARTOONS

"Raise your hand if you tripped on a tree stump on a trail run this morning but the first thing you thought of as you felt sheer pain in your knees was, Stop The Garmin! ...whew...okay, now check for blood."

Running the Jurassic Marathon

RUNNERS

WHAT MY FRIENDS THINK I DO

WHAT SOCIETY THINKS I DO

WHAT IDIOTS THINKS I DO

WHAT MY CO-WORKERS THINK I DO

WHAT I THINK I DO

WHAT I ACTUALLY DO

CHAPTER 8 - "YOU KNOW YOU'RE A RUNNER WHEN..."

These jokes are likely only funny to runners. Non-runners may not be as amused by these, but they ring true for many runners. Not only is it funny but it's incredibly true. Only a runner would laugh and go, "Yeah, so true!" So, you know you're a runner when...

- you've lost a toenail and you tell people, "It's not that bad!"
- you smirk when non-runners ask, "So how long is *this* marathon?"
- you go into Starbucks more often to use the bathroom than to buy coffee
- you get a wedding invitation and automatically think what race the date conflicts with
- you have nightmares about showing up for a race late or not wearing any clothes

YOU KNOW YOU'RE A RUNNER WHEN...

YOU PLAN YOUR RACE DAY OUTFIT MORE THAN YOUR WORKDAY OUTFIT.

YOU KNOW YOU'RE A RUNNER WHEN...

YOU PLAN YOUR SOCIAL CALENDAR AROUND YOUR TRAINING AND RACES.

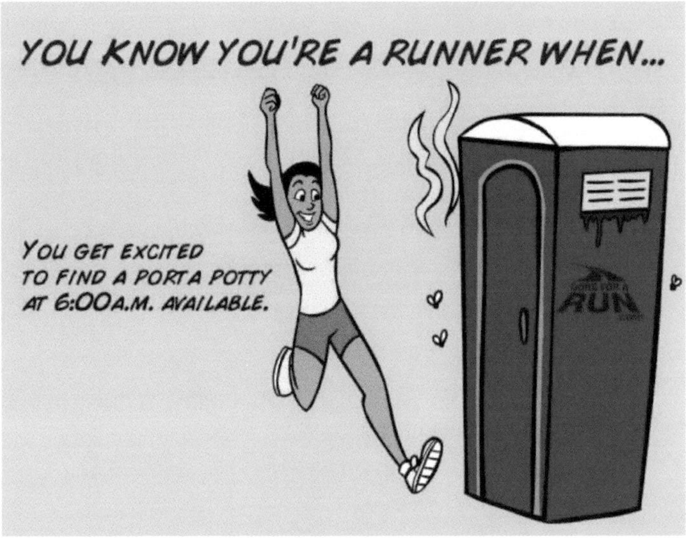
YOU KNOW YOU'RE A RUNNER WHEN...
YOU GET EXCITED TO FIND A PORTA POTTY AT 6:00A.M. AVAILABLE.
GONE FOR A RUN .com

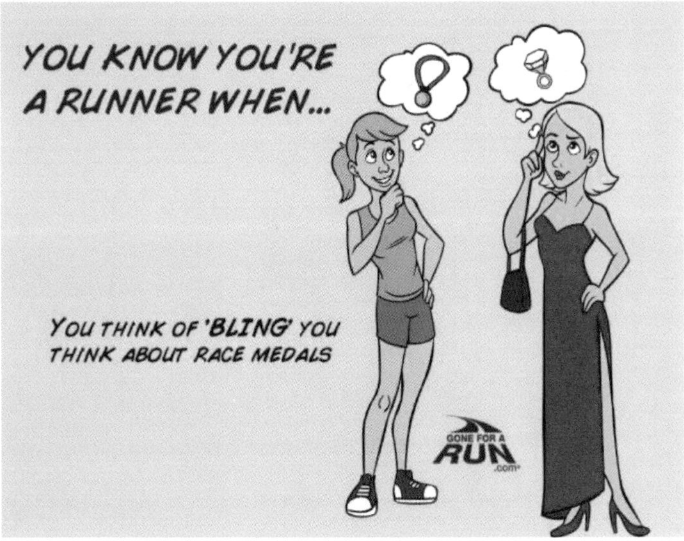
YOU KNOW YOU'RE A RUNNER WHEN...
YOU THINK OF 'BLING' YOU THINK ABOUT RACE MEDALS
GONE FOR A RUN .com

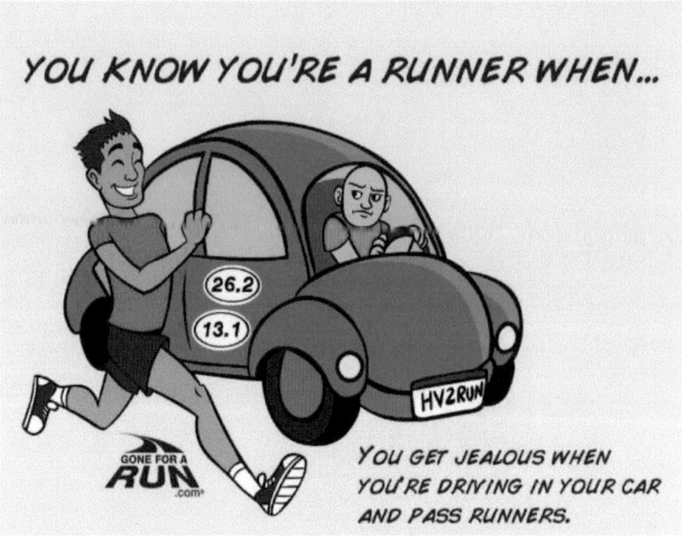
YOU KNOW YOU'RE A RUNNER WHEN...
26.2
13.1
HV2RUN
GONE FOR A RUN .com
YOU GET JEALOUS WHEN YOU'RE DRIVING IN YOUR CAR AND PASS RUNNERS.

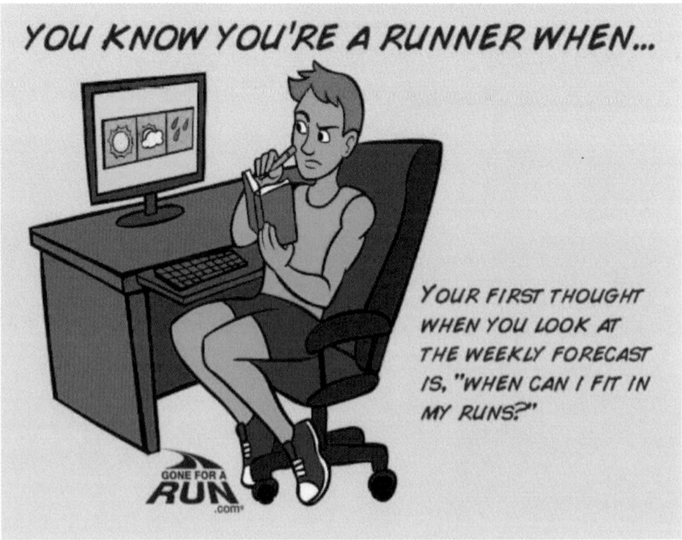
YOU KNOW YOU'RE A RUNNER WHEN...
YOUR FIRST THOUGHT WHEN YOU LOOK AT THE WEEKLY FORECAST IS, "WHEN CAN I FIT IN MY RUNS?"
GONE FOR A RUN .com

YOU KNOW YOU'RE A RUNNER WHEN...

YOU KEEP RUNNING CLOTHES AND AN EXTRA PAIR OF RUNNING SHOES IN YOUR CAR, "JUST IN CASE."

LUV2RUN

GONE FOR A RUN.com

You know you're a runner when you have more patience running over an hour than you do waiting in line at Walmart for 5 minutes.

You might be a runner if you take words such as badass, insane, freak, beast, crazy, and obsessed as compliments.

CHAPTER 9 - WHAT NOT TO SAY TO RUNNERS

Another joke list is "what not to say to runners". This is a hilarious compilation that lets everyone know what ticks runners off the most. That being said:

What not to say to runners…

- Why didn't you beat your time from last year?
- I get tired driving that far
- Running will ruin your knees!
- I did a marathon once-it was one of those 5k ones!

CHAPTER 10 - FUNNY COMMENTS MADE TO RUNNERS

Here's some adorably funny comments non-runners have said to runners:

"When I told my friend I was running a half-marathon they asked, 'Which half are you running? The first or second?'"

"I once had someone ask me, 'How long is the New York Marathon?' and I responded, 'It's a marathon…26.2 miles." And then the follow-up to that is, 'How long is the Boston Marathon?'"

"A woman I know, who by the way is a nurse, told me that running is so bad for me and said that my uterus was going to fall out. Really? I then responded to her, 'Well, then I'll just kick it to the curb and keep going. At 48 years old, I don't really need it anyway.'"

"I went into a sports shop and picked up a pair of trainers. The assistant asked if I needed help. 'I wondered if these are for overpronators,' I said. 'No madam,' replied the assistant, "they're for runners."

CHAPTER 11 - FUNNY RUNNING QUOTES

Some actual humor from actual professional runners.

"If you start to feel good during an ultra, don't worry, you'll get over it." -Gene Thibeault

"The trouble with jogging is that by the time you realize you're not in shape for it, it's too far to walk back." -Franklin Jones

"I go running when I have to. When the ice cream truck is doing sixty." -Wendy Leibman

"It's the road signs, "Beware of Lions." -Kenyan distance runner Kip Lagat, on why his country produces so many great runners

"The truth is you can always run faster, but sometimes the truth hurts!"

"I like going for runs at night because the added fear of being murdered really does wonders for my cardio."

"I like all of the things about running like eating carbs, being cheered on, and wearing comfortable shoes."

"I saw the new Jurassic World. With all of my training, I think I could run from a velociraptor for 3 seconds."

"It's not bragging when I tell you how many miles I ran today. It's so you don't judge when I devour the whole bag of chips."

"My motto is: Always run like you stole something."

CHAPTER 12 - HUMOROUS RUNNING MEMES

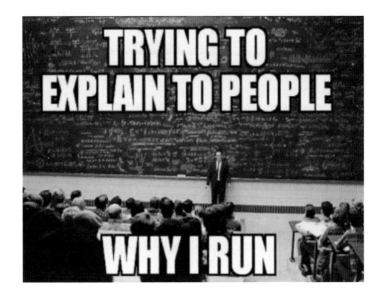

I RUN BECAUSE
PUNCHING
PEOPLE IS
FROWNED UPON

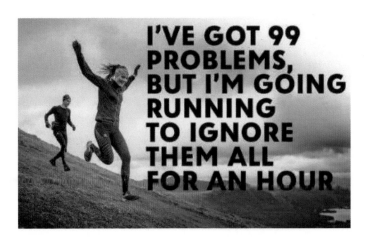

I'VE GOT 99 PROBLEMS, BUT I'M GOING RUNNING TO IGNORE THEM ALL FOR AN HOUR

I like my morning run more than I like most people.

RUNNING, CHEAPER THAN THERAPY

I wouln't say that running solves problems,

but it prevents me from causing them

NOT A RUNNER?

NOW YOU ARE

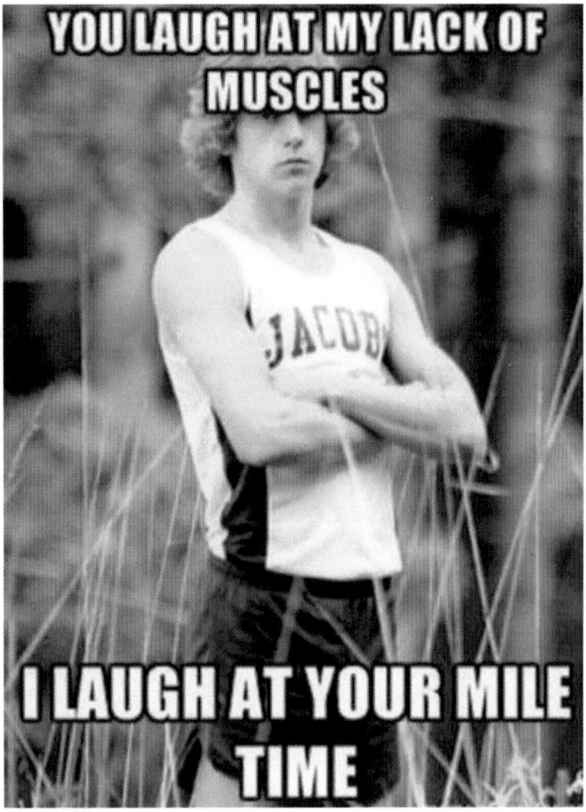
YOU LAUGH AT MY LACK OF MUSCLES
JACOB
I LAUGH AT YOUR MILE TIME

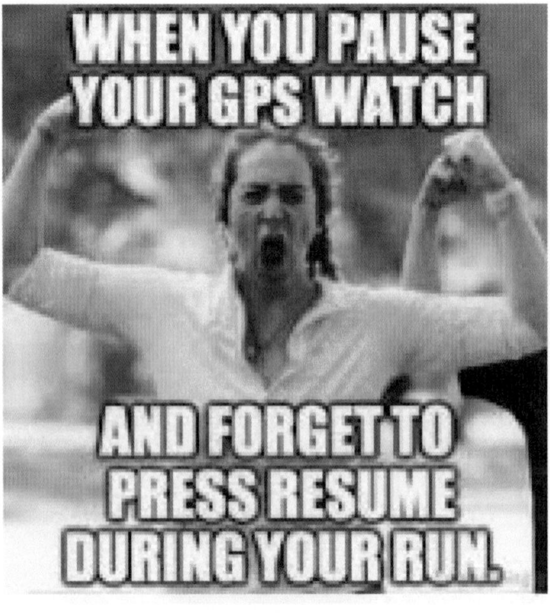
WHEN YOU PAUSE YOUR GPS WATCH
AND FORGET TO PRESS RESUME DURING YOUR RUN.

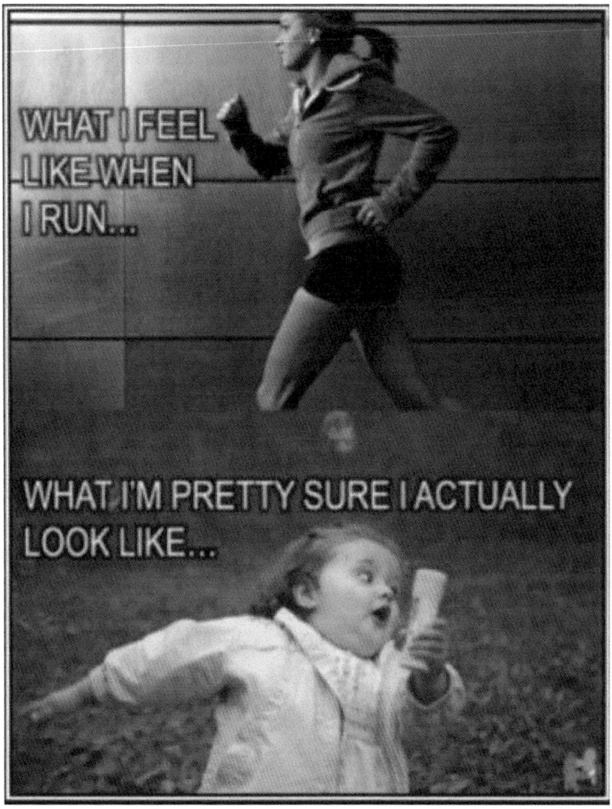
WHAT I FEEL
LIKE WHEN
I RUN...
WHAT I'M PRETTY SURE I ACTUALLY
LOOK LIKE...

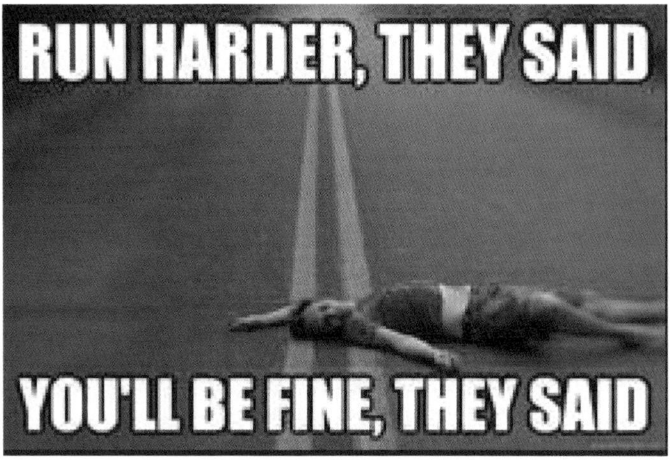
RUN HARDER, THEY SAID
YOU'LL BE FINE, THEY SAID

For someone who runs all the time, I still have the ability to make it look like it's the first time I've ever tried.

When my Grandad was 65 he started running a mile a day to keep fit.

He's 70 now and we have no idea where he is.

THIS IS A RUNNER

RUNNERS LIKE TO RUN

RUNNERS SUPPORT EACH OTHER
NO MATTER WHAT YOUR PACE IS.
RUNNERS LIKE TO ENTER RACES,
BUY RUNNING SHOES AND RUNNING GEAR.
RUNNERS ALSO LIKE TO EAT ALL THE FOOD.
THIS MAKES US HAPPY.

RUNNERS DON'T POST ANNOYING
BE LIKE BILL MEMES TO FACEBOOK
WE POST OUR RUNS TO ANNOY YOU INSTEAD.

RUNNERS ARE AWESOME.
BE A RUNNER.

IT TAKES SKILL

TO TRIP OVER
FLAT SURFACES

Run early in the morning, before your brain figures out what you're really doing.

49

Starting your day with an early morning run is a great way to make sure your day can't get any worse than it started

FACEBOOK REACTION EMOJIS EXPLAINED FOR RUNNERS

GONEFORARUN.COM

I LIKE
RUNNING

I LOVE
RUNNING

I'M
RUNNING!

I RAN
FAST

I MISS
RUNNING

I NEED
TO GO
RUNNING

CHAPTER 13 - TWEETS ACTUALLY TWEETED BY RUNNERS

1. @KevinFarzad "I'm sorry if I don't wave or smile back at you while I'm running. It's just that I'm trying very hard to not die. "
   >   5:54 PM - Dec 22, 2014

2. @KentWGraham"I hate when I'm running on the treadmill for half an hour and look down to see it's been 4 minutes."
   >   1:54 AM - Mar 30, 2017

3. @sapna "woke up in running clothes. really admire drunk me and her ambitions."
   >   5:54 PM - Dec 22, 2014

4. @chelseanachman "do people running at 6am know about not running at 6am"
   >   5:54 PM - Dec 22, 2014

5. @SortaBad [friend is telling me about running a marathon] *raises hand* "So you like did this on purpose?"

6. @laurenfleshman "That awkward moment running near a friends house when you want to text them "hey, can I poop in your bathroom real quick?"

9:40 AM - Aug 4, 2013

7. @danielhowel l"so phil and i actually just WENT FOR A RUN. i can't tell if the taste in my mouth is victory or blood from my lungs but i'll savour it."

7:52 AM - Jan 6, 2015

8. @LostCatDog*jogs for 8 minutes* *doesn't stop sweating for 14 hours*

5:38 AM - Sep 30, 2015

9. @jennyjaffe "I'm thinking of running a marathon." "Well, I'm thinking of TRAINING for a marathon. Okay, I just want to carboload."

6:55 PM - Jun 10, 2014

10. @KevinFarzad "I like going for runs at night because the added fear of being murdered really does wonders for my cardio."

10:15 PM - Jan 6, 2015

11. @KalynNicholson "Me at night: I'm getting up at 6am to run. Me next morning: maybe I'll just do a few sit-ups and call it a day.."

4:09 AM - Apr 21, 2017

12. @senderblock23 "What the fuck are we doing" - my legs during recreational jogging"

05:55 PM - 02 Jan 2014

13. @thataubbygirl"Running is great, cause you forget all your problems because you're too busy focusing on one problem, and that's that your whole body hurts."

5:57 AM - Apr 19, 2017

14. @kramediggles"I always hope that when people see me outside running they think, "wow, an athlete!" but instead it's prob more like, "Aw, good for her.""

1:36 PM - Mar 1, 2014

15. @BoobsRadley"If you ever hear me say I "love" running, I want you to sign me up for a backwards marathon down a set of spiral stairs."

8:01 AM - Feb 19, 2013

16. "Don't cry because it's over, cry because you forgot Body Glide and it's time to take a shower." -Charlie

7:01 AM - Aug 25, 2013

17. @saraschaefer1 "About to start my first half marathon and no one can tell me where the diarrhea pits are located"

7:31 AM - Oct 14, 2012

18. @HousewifeOfHell "SLAM flop boing jiggle OUCH; SLAM flop boing jiggle OUCH; SLAM flop boing jiggle OUCH; SLAM flop boing jiggle OUCH" --Me, running

7:13 AM - Mar 17, 2016

19. @IamEnidColeslaw "finally tried the whole "jogging" thing. there are people who do this every day?? for longer than ten minutes???"

6:10 PM - Oct 5, 2013

20. @AngelaEhh "Tomorrow I'm definitely going to start running, no matter how many days it takes!"

6:59 PM - Jan 3, 2017

21. @TheCatWhisprer
"ME: can't go running with you, all my workout clothes are dirty;
FRIEND: oh nice, been exercising?;
ME: no, pasta sauce"

5 :52 AM - Oct 18, 2015

22. @katiedippold"My running form could be described as "drunk woman slowly being chased by no one""

12:04 PM - Apr 13, 2011

23. @joshgondelman "I like all the things about running that aren't running. (Eating carbs, comfortable footwear, being cheered.)"

2:49 PM - Jan 2, 2013

24. @thatdutchperson "Such a beautiful day out, I thought I'd go running. But then I remembered I don't do that so now I'm eating Doritos for breakfast."

25. @IamEnidColeslaw"do people who run know that we're not food anymore"

3:51 PM - Oct 20, 2014

26. @BoobsRadley "I wish running felt great during and terrible after instead of the

reverse, because I seem to be better about doing things in vodka order."

12:30 PM - Apr 14, 2013

27. @AngelaEhh*Decides to start running again. *Bends over to tie shoes. Lol. Nope."

9:19 PM - Jun 22, 2016

DEAR READER,

Thanks for reading! If you enjoyed this book or found it useful, I'd be very grateful if you'd post a short review on Amazon. Your support really does make a difference and I read all the reviews personally so I can get your feedback and make this book even better. Thanks so much for your support.

Check out my website and subscribe to my blog at: www.tripolar.net

If you're not too busy or just bored out of your gord, then please take time to preview or read my other 2 books:

TRIPOLAR: The Story of a Bipolar Triathlete

https://www.amazon.com/TRIPOLAR-Bipolar-Triathlete-Tim-Davis-ebook/dp/B086LDKP2L

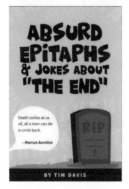

ABSURD EPITAPHS & JOKES ABOUT "THE END"

https://www.amazon.com/dp/B086BC8N5Y/ref=cm_sw_em_r_mt_awdb_EPgOEbZ24956X

RESOURCES:

http://www.jokes4us.com/sportsjokes/runningjokes.html

http://www.trainfora5k.com/running-jokes-memes/

http://www.fuelrunning.com/running/running-jokes

http://donpettygrove.blogspot.com/2014/03/top-10-run ning-jokes-i-love-running.html

http://ilovetorun.org

https://upjoke.com/marathon-jokes

http://goneforalongrun.com

https://www.goneforarun.com/funny-running-memes/1 2-funny-cartoons-about-runners.html?brand=GFAR http:// www.runnersworld.com

http://www.run100s.com/Freebies/YouKnow.html

https://www.runtothefinish.com/17-funny-running-memes/

http://runnersspirit.com/runjanerun.php

https://www.buzzfeed.com/shannonrosenberg/jogs-for-one-minute-sweats-for-five-hours

About the Author

"Ultra" Tim Davis is an avid runner and triathlete. He was born in Atlanta, GA; but raised in Wva. He moved to Los Angeles, California at age 18 to begin university. He studied many subjects in college before earning a BS in Exercise Science. He worked briefly as a personal trainer, before moving into education. He has been an athletics coach and science teacher for over 20 years. He is married with 3 children. He has completed tons of marathons, ultramarathons, and triathlons. He is a 12 time Ironman finisher, one time double ironman finisher, and 7 time 100 mile endurance run finisher. He loves to joke around with his training partners when they are out on the streets or trails, and he prefers the trails.